Undersong

Tanuja Mehrotra Wakefield

FUTURECYCLE PRESS
www.futurecycle.org

Cover artwork by Badri Nath Mehrotra; author photo by Gundi Vigfusson; cover and interior book design by Diane Kistner; PT Serif text and Sybilla Pro Condensed Light titling

Library of Congress Control Number: 2018968307

Published by FutureCycle Press
Athens, Georgia, USA

ISBN 978-1-942371-60-1

For my parents

Contents

Troubadour

Polyphonic

Weaving the Ghazal

Lullaby

Spirituals

"Such a composition has nothing to do with eternity,
the striving for greatness, brilliance—
only with the musing of a mind
one with her body, experienced fingers quietly pushing
dark against bright, silk against roughness,
pulling the tenets of life together
with no mere will to mastery,
only care for the many-lived, unending
forms in which she finds herself..."

—from Adrienne Rich's *The Dream of a Common Language*

Troubadour

Departure

My steps cut into the hill
and there my body goes,
in love with purple petals
crushed on pavement.
Why do these dead, hanging onto
the blush of life
(those petals brown too soon),
please me as they do?
All the flowers, all the trees.
If only I knew what to call things:
this explosion of mustards and pinks.
In the old house, I trace
the water-stained wallpaper with my hand,
wishing they would laugh or talk or—
sudden panic rising—one or
both could be on their way to work
in a car spinning out of bounds.
Their passing is easier to imagine
than mine. Look up, oh, the lung of it!
To alight from this russet rock like a crow,
to vanish behind clouds as water and wind
enliven the wing. The offerings here—a wizened rose,
half-eaten nectarine. I leave a purple petal
in this temple, the fruit pit not far behind.

Pilgrimage

What if I just keep walking in this single pair of shoes
along Delmar Street away from our home? What if I abandon

you with the plum trees—close the door behind me,
let it lock without a key in my pocket?

Once I endured a Boston winter with nothing
but a pair of Chinese slippers and wool socks.

I might go there again to all that's left
of fading night—my footsteps in snow.

If I passed by here years later, would you let me
stop in and see you? Or would I find a note

on the foot of the stairs, its edges curled
and on it scrawled: "Gone for a walk. Be back soon."

Love Letter

Everything to do with a white
Pomeranian and a large, pink begonia
fastened around its neck with a flourish.
Cole & Parnassus, outside the boulangerie,
the dog's fierce eyes: "Get this flower off me."
Stroll Rivoli in darkness until a streetlight illuminates
the cat tightrope-walking a chain link fence.

What fills my body with such bliss?

The winded exhilaration of climbing
hills in rain. Heart beats here and an angel
rises before me, her body carved
from a burnt-out tree: one wing bursts sky,
one leg marches Shrader into battle.
A city is made of its streets, someone said,
so I write that down. I write it.

Voyeur

Once in awhile I see the girl at the piano, her fingers buried there,
or the man sitting down to chicken and Chianti, or the television's
blue flicker on an arm or a shoulder.

More often, I'm made privy to emptiness.

Where are all the people at dusk? Under magazines, inside leather
couches, atop mahogany bookshelves. Who set tall vases of
delphinium on the table?

Am I the apparition?

Want. When looking in. Furniture nailed to the ceiling. Sex, an
argument, maybe murder. Passing by barely satisfies.

> Let's say, on the window, I'm a fly. Tiny
> wings flapping glass.

Fear and Reverie

You step into the undergrowth. A feral space. Right here, in the
midst of a manicured city at the end of a civilized street. The only
sound—your feet crushing leaves. You are quiet here and so alone.
You could disappear. No one would know, save the stalwart cats
—two of them—sentinels staring you down, unflinching. That they
might lunge, might caterwaul, might scratch, sink canines into
flesh. Quiet and alone. To disappear. Lunge, caterwaul, scratch.
Sink into flesh. A pressure in the lungs. That they might lunge.
Throb in the chest. You've felt the heart now. A muscle sore like
all the others.

Where Belgrave Ends and Shrader Begins

The cat on the stone wall moans its hello, thumps down
fatly, looking for a belly rub—scratch me, love me, here
and here. When I walk on, he mewls, zigzags, tries
to cut me off, stop me in my tracks, turn back.
Because no one wants to be left.
Not even the Papillon pipsqueak at the third floor window
whose butterfly ears flap with each yap. He prefers
my trespassing. So he can tell the sidewalk, the window,
the trees, all the deaf ears of the universe:
I'm here. Be gone! Don't leave me.

Unwell

Kitchen light. Black window:
Your reflection crunches corn chips;
mine (here for what feels like years)
sips soup. My weakened limbs
tingle at the tips, longing
to burst like buttercups in beds
of clover. The cat examines
his own green eye in the glass.

We can't see how the wind
beats the bougainvillea—
its petals pluck
and quiver, pluck
and cover, fuchsia on
the fire escape—but we hear,
in darkening descent,
a siren, a dog, a howl,
half-closed eyes, snout skyward:
one of her pack has come calling.

Strolling at Dusk

As I pass the driveway,
the canyon wind flings
his tie over his shoulder.
He tiptoes in thin dress socks
back to the car he's just parked,
rummages through the trunk
for his suit jacket and a bag of tangelos.

His feet! His black-socked feet,
shod of wing-tipped oxfords, those
bunion bruisers. Each toe pressing pavement
leaves a weary citrus scent,
a nodding-off at the wheel,
bitter coffee in the mug,
eye-watering yawn inside the quiet.
We must love the stranger.

Conversation

for Catherine

Down at the Derby Party that never happened,
dark wine pools on the parquet. You stir a mint
julep with your pinky, suck the bourbon
from the skin, ask the sprigs and me:
"How is it my father believes God loves him?"

Let's toast to a rambling house. Nothing fancy.
The kind for family. Dark green of trees and grass.
Returning to a truth: there's Kentucky cut
from you, a hillside buried with family.

But go now. Do not ask again for me
or my counsel. I am abandoned
under this sky, white clouds in wind.
When you arrive at the mountains or the sea,
will the same clouds drift in wind with no end?

Hiking Up 17th Street

—and what if
I'd read Shakespeare,
Tolstoy, Cervantes as a child?
Would the poem still be
midnight and summer
big bites of thin
roast beef slices
on white bread
washed down
with cold milk?
A sleeping house
except for me dropping
crumbs over *Anne of Avonlea,*
Emily of New Moon.
Devour the story,
swallow the sandwich—
words in the night and
right turn on Clayton.
Home now: an adult
and a vegetarian,
still reading
the Canadians.

All I Want

is a dog to saunter with me when the sky swells with color.
Her claws keep time on the pavement. Our six legs
tackle the terrain. Sniff the air. Chew whatever we dig up.
The dog could be Tiffany, if she weren't 20 years dead,
a cluster of pink warts around her eyes in the end.
Her mother, Fifi, always disappeared down dirt roads.
She comes back in my dreams, ancient and decayed,
an eyeless, lifeless corpse that suddenly resurrects.
The stocky Pekingese legs of Raja Beta and Mittuji
never walked far, while Boo always took off
for the hills. As for Benji and Daisy, Duffy,
Apollo, Lily and Puja, JR, Nacho, Newton,
Shaughnessy, Spunky and Gizmo, Abu, Guddu,
Fluffy, Luna, and Babu Sham Lal, thank you
for accepting these names, these scraps of longing.

Song for Seaglass

Amid tangled heaps of kelp,
the beach glass blooms:
honey amber, milk frost, mint green.
All salt worn and exposed.

When the sailor swigged
the last beer, when the mermaid wept
a bowl of tears, when the apothecary
and his suitcase drowned,

this glass was born.
Now we scour the sand
with our hungry fingers
for fragments, for tumbled pearls.

The heat and the tide
soften the hefty shards
into beads. Our palms fill with
miniature, misshapen, marvelous seeds.

Polyphonic

Chanda Mama

How I want to give you Hindi
flowing as swiftly as this milk,
but I can only offer *dood* or
pani, pani, pani. I'll call you
my *beti,* my *bitya rani.*
Here's *khana* and there's *aaja.*
Bolo baby bolo, I croon when
you cry. Poor Uncle Moon hangs
skyward, waiting for introductions,
thali in hand. I know not
what clatters to ground, and
maybe it doesn't matter,
as long as you drink the sound.

Nainital

a sestina

An August rain falls on Lake Naini.
How it has changed! Like the Capitol Cinema
once freshly painted white with a roof of brilliant red.
We could see the red from our school in the hills,
and between final period and dinner, sneak in a film
and from the comic shop sample Cadbury chocolates.

Collecting in our pockets so many Cadbury chocolates,
we spent our spare hours rowing boats on the lake.
Or if by some rare chance we didn't want to see a film,
we leaned against the stone balustrade outside Capitol Cinema,
watching silhouetted figures import the samba, the foxtrot to the hills,
their shadows dancing in the clubhouse whose roof was also red.

The insignia on our Biryla Mandir uniforms was not sewn in red
but in gold and purple like the wrappers of Cadbury chocolates
we littered along the steep pathways through the hills.
Hills rise on all sides around Lake Naini.
Near the flats, on the lakeshore, sits Capitol Cinema
where I saw all the musicals, my introduction to film.

An American in Paris. Suddenly Last Summer. Western films.
Elizabeth Taylor in a silk dress that must have been red,
though the film was in black and white at the Capitol Cinema.
We stopped at the comic shop for Cadbury chocolates,
which I purchased for all since my father, known in Lake Naini,
told the shopkeeper, "Keep a tab for my son who studies in those hills."

The shopkeeper nodded for all the boarding schools were in the hills.
My father did not know how much I loved to take in a film
at the cinema house towering on the shore of Lake Naini.
Since the bills came to him of so many rupees marked in red,
he did know how much I adored those Cadbury chocolates
gobbled in the dark, gazing at the lit-up screen of the Capitol Cinema.

How I found refuge in that Capitol Cinema.
Free of the chemistry textbooks awaiting me in the hills!
How can I make you see that roof of vibrant, blood red?
Fading now. Perhaps it could be recreated in a film.
All in a postcard, all in the past, what I loved of Lake Naini.
Impossible to see it or even taste it in a square of Cadbury chocolate.

I might use a filter tinted with red, if I ever made a film—
an aerial shot of Capitol Cinema from the hills. I might say, "This is
the lake, Lake Naini, Nainital, where I first tried Cadbury chocolates."

Postcard from Moradabad

Hi Mom. I'm writing you from here, a place
you called home. The mosque is still next door;
the narrow streets teem with brass makers
who shape metal into swans, fish. And more
line up at their feet—all hooves and beaks of birds.
I spy a younger you: a fistful of rupees in the heat,
buying vegetables for the family meal. Your braids
swing behind you, back and forth, tight and neat.
I can almost touch them.
Wait, I call, as you weave through the stalls
searching for the freshest *gobi,* the greenest
peas. *Wait,* while the bicycle bells peal and haul
past us, and the rising prayers never cease.

Shepherd Girl in Sari

Blackpool, England, 1967

is it full throated laughter
or a mischievous wind

that rustles her sari
chases the silk around her legs

and lifts the *pallu*
high above her head like a bird

      or a wing   or a waterfall

Mom wears a yellow sweater
on top of turquoise chiffon

a candied almond
confection puncturing

steel-gray skies and seagull cries
Daddy captures it all with his lens

three bleating sheep nudge
the oily bag of chips she holds

her slender wrist bends
to their flickering tongues

she sings them a song in Hindi
they *baah* in the Queen's English

Song for Vinyl

On a misty Thursday,
as opposed to a Gloomy Sunday,
we donate the vinyl.

No one wants the record collection—
hundreds of them, some still wrapped,
with bright orange price stickers.

No one. Not the radio station.
Not the library. Not even me?

Once a keeper of albums,
they mark my father's life. Chopin. Beethoven.
Dvorak: the bachelor in London.

Connie Francis. Johnny Mathis. Englebert Humperdinck:
a medical fellowship in Cleveland,
catching young daughters in snow.

Herb Alpert's Tijuana Brass. Frankie Yankovic
and his accordions. Crystal Gayle's hair
skimming the floor, our life settled south.

The stereophonic. Sapphire stylus. The tip radius.
The A side. The B side. The luscious size and crackle.
Smell inside a record sleeve for each discarded memory.

After hours of yes, no, maybe piles
I let them all go, like a fish and all its
shimmering scales of rainbow.

Those sonatas. This orchestra.
That philharmonic. These quartets.
A live session. A lost recording.

And all the ghazalars: Anup Jalota, Gulam Ali,
Chitra and Jagjit Singh. *Ahista, ahista.*
The *wa wa-ing* woke me on Sundays;

the sound made me mourn some
unnamable distance so I preferred
a Casey Kasem cadence, a long-distance dedication.

Dear vinyl awaiting your fate
on a humid porch, forgive me.
Forgive. Village People, Best Bossa Nova Hits! The Beach Boys.

Forgive Firebird Suite. Forgive Charles Mingus, Xanadu,
Allman Brothers, and Linda Ronstadt.
Forgive, Forgive, Forgive.

Nauratan

a cinquain series

Inside the jewelry box

Yellow
sapphires chat and
mingle with coral; pearls
cry at weddings; rubies long
for love.

"I'm keeping these for you"

This ring,
those onyx studs,
that emerald choker,
these silver anklets dipped in gold,
bangles.

Rani Haar

The queen's
necklace—patterns
of gold woven into lace
given at the time of Masi's
marriage.

So

Here is
my malachite
broach! I wondered where it
went. Was it stolen for a spell
then found?

Trinkets

Broken
clasps and stray studs.
Faded, pitied opal
and misshapen rings with cracked stones.
Discard them!

Bollywood Film Scene

Diamond
solitaire she
bit off and swallowed in
grief. It killed her instantly like
poison.

Earrings

Peacocks
with dangling tails!
Thick posts like screws widen
the earlobes, leave them throbbing with
beauty.

Nauratan

Nine gems—
to heal and soothe
adorn and offer luck
to the neck or the ear, *ithna sundar*
on a sari.

Mother to Daughter

This gold
can be melted
down and reshaped into
a bracelet or necklace or ring
for you.

Language

a sestina

Would you believe my first words were in Hindi—
munu aloo toti—a childish jibberish on my tongue.
But how sounds glint underwater: *beta, masoom, zindagi,*
discrete gems, scattered, unstrung in my heart.
Wandering through *shanti,* language of *pyar,*
I spy, leaping through a rhetorical sky, Hanuman!

Above clotheslines, clouds, trees, there soars Hanuman,
whipping his tail, longer than a song in Hindi.
Om jai jagdish hare swami jai jagdish hare. Pyar se,
she signs her letter. Sometimes sounds roll off the tongue;
other times they stumble cruelly—haven't the heart
to make themselves sensible to me. *Zindagi,*

for instance, a grand word for life, this *zindagi.*
A word belonging to a god like Hanuman,
word born under the skin, behind the ribs, of the heart—
dil. Dil se. Body beats, heart speaks pure, wild Hindi,
not this strange, broken sound cutting my tongue,
entangling *je ne sais pas* with *pyar.*

The bhajans my mother listens to express such *pyar—*
soul singing to sweet Jesus—*aachi hai mere zindagi.*
Feel *Ishwara Allah tere nam* vibrate inside my tongue,
swell the mouth as ragas ripple off Hanuman's
tail. All hairs on edge as he worships in Hindi:
Sitapati rama chandra ki? Jai! flutters in his heart.

Ragupati raghab rajaram cracks open his heart.
It overflows with love for Rama, this blood-spattered *pyar,*
for Sita finding a name for deer and demon in Hindi,
so familiar. I know I've heard them in this *zindagi*
and the lives lived before. Hindi, my liturgy; Hanuman,
my priest who wraps his monkey tail around my tongue.

Inside my mouth a universe; my fierce tongue
unfurls, licks the wounds of my battered heart,
leaps over mountains with Hanuman!
My tongue-heart says nothing, offers everlasting *pyar*.
All words are fleeting in this *zindagi*.
Someone, somewhere, teach me this Hindi.

Heart, Hanuman, Tongue, Pyar, Zindagi.
Heart-tongue, teach me this Hindi.

Song for Zion National Park

I.

Driving through bright rust
the canyon walls are a color
between orange and vermilion,
mud and fire.

A spotted owl drowning in rock.

Whirling watermarked waves
etched into stone with maidenhair fern
weeping through the cracks.

Dominion of desert and arid chaparral.
"Is it wrong to miss a brighter green?"
Daddy asks and paints on small paper.

This is how travel with family happens:
we take photographs, send postcards,
bring companions for proof.

Remember the river's roar behind the motel, will you?

II.

Food when traveling.
Fried eggs, cilantro, Tabasco.
A little savory, a little sweet.

Coffee from a shop
of taxidermied critters
unswells me.

Behind the wheel,
I nod off, try to pretend
I didn't. Stifle a yawn.

Curve after curve,
my eyelids heavy,
the sun glinting off
Mom's diamond ring.

III.

After years apart,
my parents share a room, a bed.
Daddy offers her earplugs.
She holds them in her palm
like a precious gift.

> I watch my husband
> talk with Daddy.
> Movies, music, politics.
> Once that was me
> driving through
> another mountain range.

IV.

One last pit stop, one more canyon.
My daughter mimics everything we say.
Tota pari! Daddy calls her. Little fairy.
How her fairy cries suck the living juice
out of me. How's that for love?
And it is. I know it is.
A raven punctures her
scattered crackers with its beak.
Gets while the getting is good.

Photograph: Anastasia Beach, 1975

The pier vanishes into the horizon.
A pale blue sky lies on an ink-blue sea.
We walk hand in hand to the white shack at the pier's end
with its Coca Cola sign, its lunch of battered
and fried shrimp. The breakers rush and roar.
On a radio a fisherman brought for company,
the tinny, catchy tune ensnares us.
We both have bangs and bowl cuts—
mine black, yours blonde—silky nets for sunlight.
We sip milkshakes and peer down at the wide
gaps between the wooden planks of the pier,
imagine falling into waves and rough rock.
Years must pass before I look again
and see that, yes, we held hands once
under a birdless sky. We slipped
through the slats into the sea.

Skin Hymn

Hamilton, you promised me
dung for Valentine's Day
because it would match my skin.
You said, again and again,
"You sure, really sure, you ain't black?"

From a pool of shame I tell you
I didn't want black.
I wanted the bluest eye, the blondest hair.
I took a washcloth to my knees
to scrub the color out of them.

Hamilton, you sniggered in line
behind me, with your friends,
the spit thickening on your teeth as you grinned.

Even now, a slur rises inside me:
You hambone pink-skinned scent of bacon.
Once, I chased you through the school yard,
shoved you in the back, hard.
You fell onto the grass, laughing.

Oh, I wanted to crack you with my own bare hands.

Why couldn't I find your eyes
and love the *hell* out of you?
And if there was no love to give,
why couldn't I find words?

Like:

Hamilton, my color, this brown,
is cellular: a warm sheath
of red and yellow
dung and soil, dirt and earth.
Listen for the radiance.

Weaving the Ghazal

Song for Miss Pauzer

I.

To survive, braid your days with a chorus,
make the refrain a kind of undersong.

Let each verse enter your body and hum—
be inside it. Triple tongue a kind of undersong.

Your little girl opens her mouth, and sound bubbles
fly out. She finds her own kind of undersong.

Just when you think you are home, ready to rest,
the melody turns on you—another kind of undersong.

The straight shot to joy tastes lonesome and long:
May your days fill with this kind of undersong.

Oh, Miss Pauzer, my teacher, how did you know?
A lyric is always pulsing through the vein—the undersong.

II.

To survive, braid your days with a chorus,
make the refrain a kind of undersong.

"Miss Pauzer's gotta be a werewolf with arms that hairy."
Marshmallow fluff trembles on Eric's cheek.
The lunch-time talk of fourth-grade boys.

Oh, Miss Pauzer. Your hair was feathery black.
Your skin—browner than Mrs. Cebeck.
Closer to my color. Color thought dirty.

"We came to this country on July 4th, 1969. Nakul Uncle picked us
up from LaGuardia, then drove us to a park in Brooklyn for a
barbecue. And the people were so loud! So jovial."

Let each verse enter your body and hum—
be inside it. Triple tongue a kind of undersong.

"Hey, you sure you ain't black?" Hamilton asks me. "You sure I
didn't see you on the *Soooouuuuuuul Train*?!"

Oh, Miss Pauzer. Your arm hair,
like mine, black and long. *Werewolf.*

"Happy-go-lucky. Laughing, talking. Singing songs just like back
home. They were eating the *tarbooj* with their hands. Spitting out
seeds in the grass."

Your little girl opens her mouth, and sound bubbles
fly out. She finds her own kind of undersong.

Oh, Miss Pauzer, you say songs are poems.
I play "The Dolphin Song" in your classroom.
Evan hums "Rock the Casbah" at his cubbyhole.
He will always be cooler.

You say, "Write more stories."
I am eleven and getting my period,
brown spots seeping through pink shorts.

"Can you believe? In England, I wore gloves to do grocery
shopping. But here. The people were so free."

The straight shot to joy tastes lonesome and long:
May your days fill with this kind of undersong.

I think, I need, I want a microphone.
There's always been one in my home.
For lip-synching "On the Radio," "Get Nervous," "Lucky Star."

This is dedicated to microphones rotting in garages all across America.

Home is just another exit off I-95,
a town you pass through
on your way to elsewhere.

Just when you think you are home, ready to rest,
the melody turns on you—another kind of undersong.

I don't know the flora and fauna. The juke joints.
The how and why of fried gator bits.

I do know this:

Sudarshan Uncle, sociology professor by day,
entrepreneur by night, could turn an ice rink
into a disco during that craze.
This can be done where I'm from.

Oh, Miss Pauzer, my teacher, how did you know?
A lyric is always pulsing through the vein—the undersong.

"Eating watermelon with their fingers.
That's when I knew: This was the place for me."

Song for Saint Augustine

for Nina

I.

A tall cross stands where river meets ocean.
To a child, it looked blown out to sea.

Her escapes from school were met with nun rage.
They hurled her like a stone out to sea.

Marble lions shaped my memory, waiting as the leaves
of the drawbridge groaned out to sea.

My sister and I spent years on Anastasia Beach.
We cut our toes on coquina thrown out to sea.

How many bodies did that salt water swallow?
The oldest city was built of bones out at sea.

II.

A tall cross stands where river meets ocean.
To a child, it looked blown out to sea.

We march to mass, march to mass
even me, the sole Hindu,
waiting in the last pew, hungry
to taste the wafer my friends taste.

She was unaware of sin
until they shamed her.
Damned her to hell
for *Saturday Night Fever.*

Pursed lips, rulers, stinging palms.

My sister and I spent years on Anastasia Beach.
We cut our toes on coquina thrown out to sea.

A single day back then began
with a barefoot walk to Big Joe's,
ended with the babysitter in tears
as the radio said *Elvis is dead.*

Her escapes from school were met with nun rage.
They hurled her like a stone out to sea.

"Back home in Srinagar, I became friends with two boys next
door. Father was Indian. Mother was Irish. They had all the latest
records. Frank Sinatra. Doris Day. Of course, there was Elvis
Presley. He sang so much about his baby—I used to think,
Americans must be awfully fond of children."

Marble lions shaped my memory, waiting as the leaves
of the drawbridge groaned out to sea.

Pork chops, mashed potatoes, peas
and *poori.* Mixing ketchup with mayo.
Sweet tea and *ladoos* of dahl and rice.
Who's smacking?
Sit *Indian* style, spoon sugar out of the sugar bowl.

When choosing an instrument
Mom said, *See the flute. Lord Krishna*
played that. It shined and she always
fancied things shiny and divine.

How many bodies did that salt water swallow?
The oldest city was built of bones out at sea.

Somewhere on Anastasia Island
Indians throw a party,
Krishna tastes the wafer,
and my sister wades in water
buoyant and unbound.

Torch Song

I.

Sometimes I lose my place in the sound:
A splendid, fleeting trace in the sound.

Hands like your hands—
such unsettling grace in the sound.

Your scarred hand from wrist to knuckle,
hand through wall. Waste in the sound.

Your hands, those elusive threads,
have frayed, and I'm chaste in the sound.

Try as she may to stay with you,
Tanu sees another face in the sound.

II.

Sometimes I lose my place in the sound:
A splendid, fleeting trace in the sound.

A waterlogged Norton Anthology.
You are the onion-skin pages on me.

"Why are you so far away?" she said. "And won't you ever know
that I'm in love with you, that I'm in love with you?"

Just to sit behind you in 8th period.
Just to watch your hands on the page.

A real ache, I swear. Ache.
Scoop me up, like the book.
Oh, please.

Hands like your hands—
such unsettling grace in the sound.

"My father fasted only six times in his life. Five times for each of
his daughter's weddings. The sixth time, when Gandhiji died."

That the beloved be dark and brooding.
That the love be unspoken,
not of the body but of the book left open.

To be invisible—
turn to page 365.
To be seen.

Your scarred hand from wrist to knuckle,
hand through wall. Waste in the sound.

Mash-pash, reverence, yen.
What wallflowers do.
Sit longing. Sit still. Sit.

"Please, please, please, let me, let me, let me, let me get what
I want, this time."

That he loved Cindi, then Shannon, then Jenny, then—

The ping pong pang of it. Not the kind
to think, just thought—

Your hands, those elusive threads,
have frayed, and I'm chaste in the sound.

"My mother married my father when he was eleven and she was
nine. But she did not go and live with him until she was twelve or so."

Before the taste of tongue
became as common as spitting
couplets into metal boxes. Imagine the time before.

Try as she may to stay with you,
Tanu sees another face in the sound.

"My mother collapsed into my father's arms. She actually died like that."

Song for New Orleans

A trumpet pierces the quiet on Prytania street:
music mixes with the wet, hot fill of New Orleans.

A district, a parish, a ward. A tossed sugar pie.
The tourist consumes it all, pays her bill in New Orleans.

Graves sweat above ground in the cemeteries.
Stone angels embrace their kill in New Orleans.

The sadness at his throat as he chews the hot dog bun
abandoned on a windowsill in New Orleans.

An orange offered moments before she dies,
an orb above her body growing still in New Orleans.

Leaving the quarter, I climb the levee and watch
the water, water rising against our will in New Orleans.

II.

A trumpet pierces the quiet on Prytania street:
music mixes with the wet, hot fill of New Orleans.

From an attic apartment, I watch the neighbor's gutted roof gaping
at the sky.

I watch pigeon after pigeon fly out of that hole,

the house of pigeon midwifery.

Armand,
he's tired.
So, so tired.
But he can't sleep.

The roots of a live oak crack open the sidewalk,
dancing to a fiddledeedee, funkadelic song.
The mardi gras Indian stretches his feathered wings and preens for us.

A district, a parish, a ward. A tossed sugar pie.
The tourist consumes it all, pays her bill in New Orleans.

Armand through the window.
Bluebird on a willow.
Daylight fades to yellow
but his eyes yearn green.

Birds on the windowsill taunt him;
his soft paw bats the window trim.
These days, he says, these days are grim
with many more to see.

Graves sweat above ground in the cemeteries.
Stone angels embrace their kill in New Orleans.

Wading into water up to my thighs, trying to get the car out alive.

The ferrets, Beezus and Ramona, loved to be bathed.

We are wilting on the edges of a quarter.

The window grows colder,
that bluebird sings bolder,
Armand feels much older—
How he longs to fly free!

Feline dream life, I can tell,
is deeper than a wishing well,
richer than this mortal hell
hanging from a tree.

The sadness in his throat as he chews the hot dog bun
abandoned on a windowsill in New Orleans.

Professor Ray extends a hankie and a song once sung by Fred Astaire.

It's never what we say, is it? It's *how* we say it:

to earn a living at brightness.

Armand, I'll give you birds at sea.
You do not need to comfort me.
Window is open, can't you see?
Feathers in the breeze.

An orange offered moments before she dies,
an orb above her body growing still in New Orleans.

The black woman in a pink gown gives us a tour of the plantation,

gestures toward the servant quarters, never uses the word slave.

Glass bulbs with honey catch the flies.

"That conference was the first time I went someplace without
Daddy. I was eating in a hotel and I saw they had Irish coffee.
I thought of back home with condensed milk and lots of sugar.
But this, it had a different taste. I could barely open my eyes
the next morning. But I've changed. I like that Asti Spumante.
And the margarita wine coolers. Those are really nice!"

How proudly the professor claims his ear is tin,

inhaling beignets, rollerblading, meditating, doing anything other

than hunting for traces of empire in Keats' "To Autumn."

Leaving the quarter, I climb the levee and watch
the water, water rising against our will in New Orleans.

Armand, he's tired.
So, so tired.
When will he sleep?

Dad and I stand for an hour inside that sound. Preservation of jazz, slow trombone, whirring fans. We watch the instruments talk to each other in the heat, wooden floorboards catching all that falls away. Step into the night, and Daddy says, "My God. My, my. Let's eat this ice cream."

Song for the Runner

for Steve

I.

Daylight fades, but there's still time for a run;
his figure in darkness making time for a run.

No sense in the bone-ache and the knee-crack,
passing fruit trees (six lemon, one lime) on a run.

Like poets, runners prove essential to the clan;
they rob the larder, deny the crime, then run.

The wet trail vanishes, leaves me spot-lit, blood-spirit,
tissue, sinew. Down an incline the tears run.

Let me hear those feet slapping pavement.
The body forgives painful rhyme on a run.

In a dream, I run as fast as you. In a dream, I fly.
From here to there, look at the hills I've climbed on this run.

What distance is enough? How many miles, yards, feet?
Just keep going and wake the fields of sublime on our run.

II.

Daylight fades, but there's still time for a run;
his figure in darkness making time for a run.

Most days I forget
the curl of you, the giggle—
but sometimes I feel
your warm hand on my ankle.

No sense in the bone-ache and the knee-crack,
passing fruit trees (six lemon, one lime) on a run.

A first look, a first touch,
like Danny Zuko sings, *it's electrifying!*

So one spoon nests in another.

My hair, a perpetual tangle for you,
the rest of November into December
we whispered through the snags.

Like poets, runners prove essential to the clan;
they rob the larder, deny the crime, then run.

How your body flies downhill,
the backward-turned baseball cap,
sweat beads dripping from your nose.

The wet trail vanishes, leaves me spot-lit, blood-spirit,
tissue, sinew. Down an incline the tears run.

And is it God's pleasure
or just your own,
wiping salty lips with the back of your hand
as you peel through our atmosphere?

Let me hear those feet slapping pavement.
The body forgives painful rhyme on a run.

We found each other in orbit.
But we are both exiles here,
experts at imagining elsewhere.

In a dream, I run as fast as you. In a dream, I fly.
From here to there, look at the hills I've climbed on this run.

For love runs into the beast of the other
and says, "I'll take that too."

What distance is enough? How many miles, yards, feet?
Let's keep going and wake the fields of sublime on our run.

And you'll ask me.
And I'll ask you.
How was your run?

Lullaby

She Speaks of the Tin Woodsman

He has trampled
the apples
that swirled in
the tree

and where
I was wickedly
gathering
green.

Watch him,
he is religious.
So tart
and so feverish!

Mira, Eating Berries

She forages with focus,
a snow monkey picking
at nits. Her purpling palms,
toes and knees stained
with these.

Neither straw nor rasp
nor blue but black—the tarter,
oh, the better. She uncovers
their nature like a botanist
or berry picker.

And one by one by one
Mirabai plants each
berry with a kiss
before consuming this:

> How I might
> bite those filling cheeks.
> Her hands, how they ask
> for my lips or teeth or inhale.
>
> Every bit of breath quiet, soft,
> something. When I fell, I
> couldn't stop kissing
> those cheeks.

But wonder now
at the baby, rising.
Her eyes flutter closed
with the fleeting sweetening.

Tummy Time

Let us all take
a moment to lie
on our bellies, crane
our necks, flail the arms
like so.

Now roll onto
our sides and
get stuck there.
Peddle the legs.
Cry out, cry out!
Balled fists
punch the air.

Let us scrunch up
our eyebrows
like so. Just grow
your eyes that
wide. Just try.

Toes

I find you. Threading your toes through air. Cautiously, you examine the nubs. Look at that. There, where they've always been. But to discover them. For the first time. Like a word in a poem that wasn't there before. Gimcrack. Or acanthus. Those little piggies wiggle under your dominion. What's it like? To make your toes part the air for that first time. I can't remember. You won't remember either, even if I am your witness.

Birdsong

You alight on a picket fence and cock your head
at this lawn of seemingly indistinguishable green or
closer, with your bird eye, note its sharp, yellow, uneven blades.
Your cry pierces the rain; the wind rattles the gate—
slamming open and shut, open and shut.
Just along for the ride—this family you're born into.
One day you will walk to the mailbox,
hot concrete soaking into your feathers.
I am grateful for big windows to watch you.
What am I to teach you?
Help me understand where you come from.
And here you are.
Your sweet mouth always smelling of milk.

Garden

(for Mira and June)

If I build you a bower
of willow to spill over and swing upon
or a maze of high-walled stone
for hiding, and I show you how
earthworms shine in the sun when unearthed,
would you entwine like the jasmine vine?

If I help you steady the shovel, dig deeply
in the dirt so that it blooms under your
fingernails, or let you wander barefoot
over rocks, eat marigold petals, save
all the deadheads, sip sand, get stung,
would you roll each other down this hill forever?

If I left you alone in this suburban
silhouette of grass and flower bed,
would you cleave together through
drought and rain, wind and sun?
Would you eat from the same apple?

Tooth Song

After school, she runs to show me
her newly lost baby tooth—
still bloody and alive,
it leaps from her hands to my hands
to the flagpole in the grass
hiding amid blades of green.

A crowd gathers—curious children,
woeful mothers who cluck:
"Ah, well. Let it grow into a tooth tree."

Like hell.
We can find clear beads,
Lego bits, glitter in sand;
we can find this.

On my hands and knees now, I rake
and paw the grass, searching
for a tooth to be kept, not left to any fairy
for a coin. She'll give other teeth,

but she wants to hold
this one forever—or at least
until Christmas when
elves come collecting.

I bounce up, my hand above me,
pressed between my index finger and thumb—
her precious bone kernel,
hollow and sharp like a slivered almond
or cracked pearl.

Playdate

Some days I don't want to host little children in my house. Feed them my food. Tell them my rules. I want to fling the doors open and say "Go play!" There. See the little bodies line up and climb aboard a flying carpet of green. It should fit at least ten and hover above all stranger danger. But let it touch down once in awhile. Let them disembark. May they uncover a mystery I am not privy to, like a creek behind the last house on Southwind Circle. May they score flower-shaped cookies covered in sweet-white icing from Mrs. Bergman. May Laura Hern's twirling baton whirl in their ears. Sand burrs on socks. Sucking on the scabs of mosquito bites. And when they scramble up the magnolia tree into unending sunlight, may it blind them with glory.

God's Eyes

We twist yarn around
two popsicle sticks held together
in the shape of a cross.

Under and over, over and under—
a pattern of color accretes
into diamond or square,

into crucifix or plus sign or owl's eye,
depending on your persuasion.
The six-year-old tugs feverishly

at her vision of coasters;
the two-year-old wraps hers
into a bubbling knot she carries to bed.

Quiet creeps through the house.
Turning the wool with my fingers,
I am a stick weaver in the night.

'Tis the Season

Are you listening? The night we caught a seven-foot tall tree
in a green net, it was noisy more than silent, full of rattled voices
belting "Jingle Bells" off key.

Do you hear what I hear? We sang *fa la la la la* and *Batman smells,*
drove winter wonderland all the way home, soon breathing in that
wet pine scent, those daughters murmuring in sleep.

Hark, hark the bells—sweet and silver noble fir—unnetted and
naked now in the window, waiting for sparkles, for ornamentation.
Were the four birds *colly* or *calling*?

When else can we sing *glisten, glory, partridge* and *cheer* with
such abandon? The tree glimmers. "So beautiful," we gasp over a
thing dying. And only now, this one time of year, I long to believe

in a holy child and kneel in the church pew,
sighing under the weight of song.
One daughter awakens —"Did Santa come already?"

No way baby. We've only just begun.
My voice always chokes on the final
pa rumpa pum pum.

I am a little poor boy too who forgets the lyrics,
wanders into blue-green silence,
pine needles dropping daily on the crisp tree skirt.

Book of Kells

(Trinity College, Dublin, 2002)

We peer at pages
under glass:
letters drop-capped,
illuminated.

Book of calfskins—
hundreds and hundreds
of them—flesh boiled,
peeled and bleached.

Run your fingers
across parchment,
past pores where
hairs have been
circling the divine
word on skin.

And dare not think
on the red ink—
vermilion dye—
extracted by crushing
pregnant insects.

Song for the Zamboni

All afternoon we flail
on the hard grooves
that catch our skates.

Then you arrive with a hum
and glide around the rink,
bewitching us.

You dissolve all our scores,
resurfacing the ice into
a wet fluorescent stone.

From the sidelines, we long
to rush the freshened rink
that begs us to mark it.

But now we wait
as you revive the well-worn ice
with a blade and a watery glaze.

Bubblegum Classic

An uncle tells me: "Try
sweetening your tea with juice
from a plump grape."

But why wean myself from the sugar
teat, from chocolate
truffle, peppermint, crème-filled.
How gorgeous the blood rush!

What of a little buzz in my blood?
We all pick our poisons.
I'll mull. I'll dulcify.
Anyone would
when the tongue
is laid bare and lonely
waiting for the tingle.

The Chipmunks Genuflect to Me

We are made
of yellow brick
and ruby slippers.

We believe some
entity will fill us,
be it brains, fries
or domestic bliss.

You think Toto
longs for home too.

I think the little dog
wants to keep
sniffing that green
whiff of witch.

But I won't tell you that.
Not no how!

I could be wrong.

Maybe a decent—no,
a dazzling—pair
of shoes can
guide us.

There's heart, home, nerve
tucked inside the toe box.

Spirituals

Good Friday in Wicklow

We wander onto a beach of stones: greens and purples, veined
with color, smoothed by the sea. Here's a gray one, striped white
right through the middle, as if someone put it there.
Breathless in the wind, you take it from me. "Watch this,"
you say; flick your wrist, skim my stone. It dips, then bounces,
then sinks into dark water. Before I can say "Wait," you skim another
and another—a disk of rust, a palm-sized paperweight of jade.
"Flat ones are the trick," you say, "Secret's in the spin."
A stone flies, skipping seven times. It walks on water, alive
for a moment, before it drowns. Your delicate hands, small
as a boy's. And like the pink flush of skin, blue-tinged
lips; the Irish sea rushes to Candlewood Lake, Connecticut, 1972.
You skim another and another through time and water,
while I stand beside you, filling my mouth with stones.

By Whose Gracious Light?

Five Haibun

1.

That she might really find a wocket in her pocket. Something green
peering out of denim blue. Rhyme knits language like a scarf, and
we turn pages together. Watch dying trees shimmer in riverbeds.

> house floats on a mouse
> lotus vibrates with locust
> wet rippling planes

2.

Driving through St. Francis Woods, I say, "To live on St. Elmo
Street! His intestines were yanked out of his body and spooled.
Besides, it's also that bad movie, that dreadful saxophone theme."
He says, "But if you were a kid—Elmo's practically a saint
anyway, isn't he?"

> puppet or sailor
> some laughter lasts for ages
> furry, water, plight

3.

A chosen day for worries: to make dinner, poems, money, and
cufflinks from buttons. Sworn to secrecy, avoiding torture, the ants
construct miracles with crumbs. Bready ones work best. At this
luxurious moment of pen to paper, another body is blown to bits
or burned or burrowed into with a sharp object.
By whose gracious light am I spared?

> warm midnight simmers
> birds caught, flutterless, flightless
> eyes open in sleep

4.

Hand. Foot. Mouth. Some disease. A flu succumbs to red
rashes on mouth, foot, hand. Delicate immunities. "The
Upanishads are too abstract sometimes," Mom says. "Wayne
Dyer really explains it best." Krishna and Arjuna ride close in
the chariot. Did they share a fruit, a foot, a hand? Maybe
guava. Maybe loquat. Flowering of the tree, petals all over me.
It's twenty years since I've seen India.

> Traveling westward
> a divine U-turn in snow
> brings me home to you

5.

Green beans boil like whirling dervishes in water. Hope: My daughter
will eat and finally poop. When her body opens, my body opens too.
So motherhood marches past beer-bottle glass on a sidewalk.
Sunlight, the dappled kind, illuminates this page, then leads my
hand into darkness.

> She says *friendboy*
> and the world electrifies:
> brilliant little pearls

Belle Monti

On this mountain our streets curve
and dead-end when we least expect it:
fog-filtered sunlight, green-leaf flicker.
Children brace themselves against wind
lugging backpacks up the avenue of fleas,
while deer eat from our gardens, our palms—
their black eyes rooted inside us.
We share the wine, quarrel like crows
over traffic, permits, plots of land.
When a neighbor dies without reason,
we carry the weight as if he were our own,
pray for every squirrel in the road.
We fish the streams, name the streets,
nurse the baby, collect our quiet histories.
And we too will leave a trace on this mountain.

Diya

Some say *festival of lights,*
others say *Indian New Year* or *death of a ten-headed demon God*
or *defeating darkness in each human heart.*

It depends on who you ask.

But there is always the *diya,*
little lamp we light with a flame
and set on balconies, windows, and walkways.

Think of Ram and Sita
turning to face Ayodhya after a long exile.
What was it like

to leave the dark wood
and find their distant kingdom
lit with lamps to welcome them home?

Home, on the verge of burning,
that flickering wing of light
ready to ravage all.

Think of the reflection
in Sita's brown eyes, her footsteps
illuminating the earth.

Think of homecomings—how far I am
from mine, how much farther my mother is
from hers. And you, are you home?

If not, no matter—
we are like Sita, in shadow,
believing the lamp-lit walk means all.

Ichetucknee Springs

For Mintu (Feb 25, 1973 to May 13, 2016)

Black inner tubes carried us down that river,
remember? Through that cold, luminous water
whose quick currents hurtled us over

fallen cypress trees, whose branches reached for us.
The water gleamed silver and clear as it consumed
Mom's sunglasses, Uncle's wallet, the car keys.

We might return to where we were before,
but we'd have to swim upstream,
grab hold of gnarled tree knobs, and *pull* our way up.

Remember: our parents climbed clumsily into rafts—
so few could swim—threaded their fingers
through the water, laughed so loudly together.

No news scrawled on a blue aerogramme
from brother or mother or another country
could be missed, not that day.

Remember: that snake coiled on an aching tree branch,
reaching for Aunty who plunged into the river
with a shriek and thrashed wildly in the water?

Uncle tried to lift her, but her arms
were like tentacles wrapped
around his neck, dragging him under.

Remember splashing, then silence.
Beads of water on brown skin.
Breathing.

Uncle burst from the river's surface,
a baptized man, with Aunty in his arms,
choking on sweet air, delivering salvation.

Remember: our boredom,
so we threw down a challenge—
abandon the inner tubes, go faster, swim it!

We kicked the cold stream with a fury,
flew away from their cries
to be careful, go slow.

Not our tribe. Underwater
we loved the muted sound, how the light
rained down on bright green reeds and that glimmering.

Above us, the Spanish moss,
the sun behind the clouds;
the water turned our skin to scales and gills.

For a moment, we were a school of fish
iridescing, flowing, and flown.

Ditty

Simmer every sour threat they throw
at you! Circumvent the sauces
and the coarsely chopped.

Melt into a skillet sometimes.

Be wary of medium heat. Play
coy with graters, shredders,
processors, mixers of all sorts.

This is necessary for survival.

Find yourself on the verge
of being minced, zested, or blanched?
Pray for it to be short, wet, and flavorful.

Succumb, if you must, to your disintegration,
but only in that final journey from plate
to lips to tender, consuming tongue.

The Logical Song

If the extension cord under the dresser
turns its serpent eyes on me
and flickers its pronged tongue

if the bone burns red and
hot to the touch and begs for nothing
but a joint replacement

if the bluejack spears his beak
into a Cadbury egg
and carries it into oblivion

if the pine, if the fir
is dislodged from ancient
hiding places

then I am with you
examining our problem
side by side, under a single lupe.

If there are children
among us who ask
what is pillage, what is infection

if the caterpillar escapes
the flower plucked
for teacher appreciation day

and crawls with slow determination
down the white picket fence
displaced from petal to wood

if girls on the lake
build a raft with
such fresh green reeds

and if the collection includes
hawk feather, walnut half
star-studded sky
then I am with you.

December Lament

Is it the seasonal chill, rain for some, snow for others, the memory
of something lost, that makes this day so?

A child is born who will later be crucified, and we all know it.
And so rejoicing sounds close to mourning.

You can hear the melancholy everywhere—in Schroeder's fingers
buried at the piano, in the multitudinous choir, in the divine night,
in the ringing of a single bell.

Songster

The materials are here before me—
paper, pen, keyboard, screen
skin tone, color, desolation
sense, smoldering, illness
cantankerous.
These words stretch
out like the days do, asking for
organization, for attention.
Like wind and rain
roaring through night hours,
they come and come,
leaving everything wet with excess.
Too many nuts and chews,
an everflowing bottle of wine.
Always such shameful
plenty: toothpaste that never runs out—
neither the toilet paper
nor the milk, neither the coffee
nor vigor and succor—
useful words too
so the poems,
like the goods,
regenerate miraculously.

Sparkler

With one match, this long gray stick
bursts into tiny, persistent glints
like a baby's sudden tears,
and wiry lines of orange light
buzz and glow, streak the sky.
I brandish this wizard wand,
making loop de loops through the air,
spelling out my name with flame
that always dies too soon.
But in the smoke-thick sadness
I find another stick,
touch it to another flame,
and *whoosh*
I am reaching for you
with these fingertips of fire

girl and spark—

Notes

Conversation: This poem was inspired by Wang Wei's poem "To See a Friend Off"

Chanda Mama: The title is taken from the first lines of a lullaby sung in Hindi about a loving Uncle Moon up in the sky eating and sharing his food from a big silver plate, *a thali.*

Nainital: Nainital is a hill station in India where the British colonists would spend the summers to escape the heat. It was also the location for numerous boarding schools in India, like the one for Indian boys referred to in the poem, called *Biryla Mandir.*

Nauratan: Nauratan is a jewelry set, usually a necklace, earrings and a ring made from nine gemstones and laid in gold. This kind of jewelry would often be part of an Indian bride's dowry. These poems are a series of nine cinquain.

Weaving the Ghazal: The poems in this section of the book are in a form I invented. I write a ghazal in English and then I weave the couplets of that ghazal into another poem that contains song lyrics, tercets, quatrains, blues stanzas, and quotation.

Torch Song: Lyrics have been woven into the poem from the songs, "Just Like Heaven" by the Cure and "Please Let Me Get What I Want" by the Smiths.

She Speaks of the Tin Woodsman: This poem is a homosyntactic translation of William Carlos Williams' "This Is Just to Say."

The Chipmunks Genuflect to Me: The title and italicized text come from the song, "If I Were King of the Forest" performed by the cowardly Lion in *The Wizard of Oz.*

By Whose Gracious Light: The haiku at the end of haibun 5 echoes a phrase from "Geronition" by T. S. Eliot: "Thoughts of a dry brain in a dry season."

Ichetucknee Springs: The last line echoes a line from "At the Fishhouses" by Elizabeth Bishop: "Our knowledge is historical, flowing, and flown."

Acknowledgments

Versions of these poems first appeared in the following literary journals:

The Alembic: "Chanda Mama"
The Asian Pacific American Journal: "Nainital"
Chicago Quarterly Review: "Song for St. Agnes," "Threading the Ghazal"
Dogwood Journal of Poetry and Prose: "Book of Kells"
Ellipsis: "Garden"
Fourteen Hills: "Geological Knowledge"
Ki'in: "Anastasia State Park"
Petrichor Machine: "Mira, Eating Berries," "Love Letter"
Solstice Literary Magazine: "Torch Song" (Stephen Dunn Poetry Award
    Finalist)
Transfer: "She Speaks of the Woodsman," "Pilgrimage," "Fear,"
    "Language"

"Song for New Orleans" appeared in *Indivisible: An Anthology of Contemporary South Asian American Poetry* (University of Arkansas Press, 2010)

I'd like to express my deepest gratitude to my parents, Drs. Pushpa and Badri Mehrotra, for their love and encouragement. Their voices can be heard throughout this collection. Special thanks to Steve, Mira, and June Wakefield for their unwavering love, patience, and support; to Nina Kurup, for being there through everything; to Sarah Bardeen and Athena Kashyap, whose generous feedback and insightful edits have made these poems what they are; to Lisa Rosenberg who helped me shape the book in its final stages; and to all my family and friends who have supported me on this poetry-making marathon. Thanks as well to my teachers— Toni Mirosevich, Nona Caspers, Paul Hoover, Margaret Cezair-Thompson, and Frank Bidart—who showed me all the many things a poem can do, and to Kathleen Beasley, Stephanie Vargas, and the city council of Belmont for allowing me to be the poet laureate of our town for three years; the experience was transformative. A huge thank you to Diane Kistner for her skillful editing, her patience with me, and her "no-nonsense" approach to making this book. Finally, I'd like to thank Elizabeth Bishop for *At the Fishhouses*; Lucille Clifton for *Cruelty*; Mark Doty for *A Display of Mackerel*; Seamus Heaney for *Digging*; Emily Dickinson for *I Am Nobody*; and all the other makers whose poems sustain me.

About FutureCycle Press

FutureCycle Press is dedicated to publishing lasting English-language poetry books, chapbooks, and anthologies in both print-on-demand and Kindle ebook formats. Founded in 2007 by long-time independent editor/publishers and partners Diane Kistner and Robert S. King, the press incorporated as a nonprofit in 2012. A number of our editors are distinguished poets and writers in their own right, and we have been actively involved in the small press movement going back to the early seventies.

The FutureCycle Poetry Book Prize and honorarium is awarded annually for the best full-length volume of poetry we publish in a calendar year. Introduced in 2013, our Good Works projects are anthologies devoted to issues of universal significance, with all proceeds donated to a related worthy cause. Our Selected Poems series highlights contemporary poets with a substantial body of work to their credit; with this series we strive to resurrect work that has had limited distribution and is now out of print.

We are dedicated to giving all of the authors we publish the care their work deserves, making our catalog of titles the most diverse and distinguished it can be, and paying forward any earnings to fund more great books.

We've learned a few things about independent publishing over the years. We've also evolved a unique, resilient publishing model that allows us to focus mainly on vetting and preserving for posterity poetry collections of exceptional quality without becoming overwhelmed with bookkeeping and mailing, fundraising activities, or taxing editorial and production "bubbles." To find out more about what we are doing, come see us at www.futurecycle.org.

The FutureCycle Poetry Book Prize

All full-length volumes of poetry published by FutureCycle Press in a given calendar year are considered for the annual FutureCycle Poetry Book Prize. This allows us to consider each submission on its own merits, outside of the context of a contest. Too, the judges see the finished book, which will have benefitted from the beautiful book design and strong editorial gloss we are famous for.

The book ranked the best in judging is announced as the prize-winner in the subsequent year. There is no fixed monetary award; instead, the winning poet receives an honorarium of 20% of the total net royalties from all poetry books and chapbooks the press sold online in the year the winning book was published. The winner is also accorded the honor of being on the panel of judges for the next year's competition; all judges receive copies of all contending books to keep for their personal library.

Made in the USA
Middletown, DE
23 February 2019